M000046872

ELEVATION

ELEVATION

FRED LOUIS

Trilogy Christian Publishers A Wholly Owned Subsidary of Trinity Broadcasting Network

2442 Michelle Drive Tustin, CA 92780

Copyright © 2020 by Fred Louis

Scripture quotations marked (NKJV) are taken from the *New King James Version*®. Copyright © 1982 by Thomas Nelson, Inc. Used by permission. All rights reserved.

No part of this book may be reproduced, stored in a retrieval system or transmitted by any means without written permission from the author. All rights reserved. Printed in USA.

Rights Department, 2442 Michelle Drive, Tustin, CA 92780.

Trilogy Christian Publishing/ TBN and colophon are trademarks of Trinity Broadcasting Network.

For information about special discounts for bulk purchases, please contact Trilogy Christian Publishing.

Trilogy Disclaimer: The views and content expressed in this book are those of the author and may not necessarily reflect the views and doctrine of Trilogy Christian Publishing or the Trinity Broadcasting Network.

Manufactured in the United States of America

10 9 8 7 6 5 4 3 2 1

Library of Congress Cataloging-in-Publication Data is available.

ISBN: 978-1-64088-969-9

E-ISBN: 978-1-64088-970-5

Dedication

To my loving and caring heavenly Father, my Lord and King Jesus Christ, and my Helper and Best Friend the Holy Spirit. Lord, I will love You more than I will ever love any human being, forever, in Jesus' name. May my life forever bring You glory.

To my lovely wife, Prophetess Naomi Louis, and adorable son, Joel Louis. You two are my inspiration and the reason I push so hard.

Prophetess Naomi: after God, I would not be who I am without you. You believed in me and stuck with me, even when it meant you making sacrifices for me. You are my Queen. It's hard to really express myself about you, because I will always feel like crying. You're my best friend, you're the answer to my prayers, you're my inspiration in ministry, you're my gorgeous beauty, and you're simply my dream Proverbs 31 wife. Our marriage has eternal kingdom purpose, and together we won't compromise our assignment, anointing, and approach unto God for anyone, in Jesus' name. My love, you make the bitter moments of life sweet. You are the most powerful preacher, praise and worship leader, and intercessor I know. I love you, tutu mwen.

Joel: I will always be there for you. May this book inspire you to walk in your elevation from a young age, in Jesus' name. Your life is destined from God for greatness. My desire is for you to double all that I do in the Lord. You make my life so joyful, even as a young boy. I will never be a dad who will walk out your life—never. When you get older, may you read this book and continue in the mantle on my life and outdo all that I do. I love you, Jojo, with all my heart. Daddy will always protect you and have your back. I truly can't wait to see the supernatural, great works the Lord will do in your life. I declare on your life that you will walk in divine health and wealth, in the power of the Holy Spirit, and with great kingdom authority over the enemy. Every day, Daddy will always pray for you and speak only greatness over your life. Never doubt Daddy's love for you, my support for you, and me being proud of you. You are a powerhouse for Jesus, and I declare that you shall serve the Lord in greatness all the days of your life, in Jesus' name.

To my mom, whom I have no words for: you are the strongest mother I know. I've seen you in every season, and you have given me a true example of how to make it in life. I honor you, Mom, and I love you.

To my sister, Anna: I'm so proud of you and am inspired by your hard work. As your big brother, I will always be there for you.

In honor of my father, who died when I was sixteen. I thank you, Lord, for keeping me, my mom, and my sister through hard times.

Mom and Anna: may you two walk in elevation from the Lord, in Jesus' name. Thank you all for supporting my assignment from King Jesus.

Table of Contents

Acknowledgements

Jonathon Mallory

Willeta Brown

Miguel Delgado (Freedom House Investments)

Noelle Govender (C Govender & Associates CC,
& Baca Commodities (PTY) LTD)

Peggy Lingrand (Fit2Healthy4Life)

Marie Jackson

Elsie Akogo

Introduction

The desire of every up-and-coming leader is to be elevated by God—for God to be so pleased with you that He would count you worthy to be recognized in heaven and among His people. Elevation means to lift up or make higher in rank or status. In the kingdom of God, elevation comes only from God. Elevation is when God publicly establishes you as His leader for His people. Elevation affects your finances, your name, your status, your respect, your gifting, your access, your anointing, your family, and even your seed. When God Himself elevates you, it will even make the most famous, wealthy, or worldly individual envy you. You cannot be elevated by God and it be a secret. Elevation from God will influence your capacity to make an impact. It brings a host of benefits and challenges. There's joy and jealousy all at the same time. There's opulence and opposition simultaneously. Can you handle all that comes along with elevation? Yet, one important truth and revelation that our generation has skipped over is that elevation is a process. It does not happen overnight. There are immovable kingdom principles that govern the reality of elevation. Elevation is not a prophecy. It's a process.

Whether you are a minister, entrepreneur, doctor, school teacher, student in school, or a stay-at-home mom, elevation is for you. It's something we are all looking for and dreaming of, but don't know how to experience. What we call elevation, the Bible calls the Promised Land. The Promised Land is not heaven, as many people believe, because the children of Israel fought thirty-one kings before possessing the Promised Land, and we know that in heaven there is no fighting at all. So, then, what is the Promised Land? The Promised Land is complete rest. What do I mean? Yes, elevation is when your name becomes great, when you are recognized publicly, when you are financially prosperous, and when you have undeniable influence, but all of this is wrapped up in one word: rest. Let me explain. Nobody becomes chief executive officer (CEO) of a company overnight; it's a process. You work your way up from the bottom to the top. In other words, elevation is coming from a place of private insignificance to public prominence. No matter what season of life you are in, your calling from God can make you feel like all you do is battle every week, and there's no end to the resistance of life.

In Scripture, David felt the same way. David went from one battle to the next. Yet the moment of elevation finally came for David in 2 Samuel 7:1 (NKJV). "Now it came to pass when the king was dwelling in his house, and the LORD had given him rest from all his enemies all around." This is what elevation looks like. Here is good news: there is coming a time in your life when the spiritual battles to get to your place of elevation will end, and you will rest in your place of influence from God. The reason why it's so hard is because your promised land of elevation has spiritual enemies in all shapes and forms, fighting you tirelessly day and night to keep you from this elevation or rest. These enemies can include your family, friends, co-workers, church members, and anyone who blatantly tries to oppose your elevation, either by their thought-provoking words, actions, or subliminal messages. Therefore, the apostle Paul states in 1 Corinthians 16:9 (NKJV), "For a great and effective door has opened to me, and there are many adversaries." Not only is the door already there for you; it's a great one—but the problem is that you have adversaries prohibiting you from entering that rest. Solomon said in Ecclesiastes 3:1 (NKJV), "To everything there is a season, a time for every purpose under heaven." The author of Hebrews puts it this way in Hebrews 4:9 (NKJV), "There remains therefore a rest for the people of God."

Wherever you are in life right now, no matter what season you are in with your calling, there are specific kingdom principles you must follow to experience elevation. Whether you are a student in Bible college or anointed from God for the marketplace, in this book you will find in-depth spiritual keys to unlock your access to your promised land of elevation. The Bible is a book about God elevating different men and women from all walks of life. God elevated prime ministers, kings, prophets, priests, queens, fivefold ministry leaders, army generals, judges, widows, orphans, poor men, and the wealthy. God elevates ordinary people—those who are overlooked and rejected from every facet of life. No matter where you are all over the world, no matter your calling or purpose on the earth, this book will teach you how to go from where you are now to the place of elevation God has predestined for you. I will be teaching you from the life of Joshua, but the Holy Spirit will speak specifically to you where you are to help you get to the next level. It takes prophetic revelation in four areas: Mantles, Manifestation, Might, and Miracles. Revelation creates acceleration to your divine destination. You are not going to be fighting and battling for the rest of your life. After reading this book, you will be positioned to possess your promised land of elevation.

Chapter 1

RECEIVING A SUPERNATURAL MANTLE

There are few people in the body of Christ who truly flow in a genuine mantle. It's a term that circulates a lot, but a true mantle is rare! A real mantle is more valuable than money, publicity, and connections. In a time when many desire to go to the next level, reach the nations, become a household name, and have a big ministry, somewhere in all of this we have lost what it takes to be a powerful man or woman of God! The reality is that most people do not have the character to be a Moses, a David, an Elijah, or a Joshua. When God was choosing the new king of Israel after Saul, God put a high demand on character by declaring that He looks at the heart. In this chapter we are going to discover what qualified Joshua, out of millions of Israelites, to replace and carry the mantle of a once-in-a-lifetime prophet by the name of Moses.

What is a mantle? The word "mantle" is an English translation of the Hebrew word "addereth." Before I break down the meaning of this term, I want to share with you a definition I received in silent prayer. A mantle is "a distinct anointing of the Holy Spirit upon a person that only that individual operates in." This is very important, because if what you're operating in others are doing as well, it's not a mantle. It's a ministry! John the Baptist attracted civilized Israelite citizens into an uncivilized, uncomfortable wilderness, because no one was saying the things John the Baptist was saying, for he was distinctly "the voice crying out in the wilderness." "Distinct" means a recognizable difference. Think about this: out of all the qualified soldiers of King Saul who could have responded to the disrespectful challenge of Goliath, why was it only David that not only responded to

Goliath, but lopped his head off? The answer is in the chapter before: David received a mantle, a distinct anointing of the Holy Spirit, that only he could fight and kill the Philistine giant! Where were the other prophets when Ahab was rising to become the most wicked king in Israel? Elijah had a rare, unusual, distinct mantle that only he could confront Ahab and write a check that only he could cash. When you have a mantle, you can back up audacious declarations! A mantle sets you apart and makes you instantly in human demand, because you don't preach, sing, teach, prophesy, and operate in miracles like others. A mantle can be described in seven ways.

Garment

A mantle was a garment that was worn in biblical times. When the kingdom was torn from King Saul, he tore the mantle or garment of Prophet Samuel, to which Samuel prophetically declared that Israel would be torn from him in the same manner. Psalm 109:29 (NKJV) says, "Let my accusers be clothed with shame, and let them cover themselves with their own disgrace as with a mantle." It was part of the everyday life of the children of Israel. Yet there were a few prophets who would wear, as a garment, the very anointing of God upon them everywhere they went. As a matter of fact, when King Saul requested the witch of Endor to raise Samuel from the dead, what caused Saul to perceive that it was Samuel was that he was covered with a mantle, even in the supernatural realm. A prophet who has a true mantle carries this distinct anointing everywhere. Jesus would do most of His miracles outside of a synagogue. They brought sick people in beds into the streets, with the hopes that the shadow of Peter's mantle would fall upon them to heal them. It's a garment, because you wear a garment everywhere you go, which speaks of being able to operate at a high level in the Spirit everywhere you go. Something is wrong if miracles only happen in your ministry behind the pulpit. Just like you are dressed in a shirt, this mantle rests upon you, even when you are not trying to minister. Jesus just came off the boat, and a demon-possessed man was begging Him for mercy. The dead bones of Elisha raised a man from the dead, because he had Elijah's mantle.

Glory

A mantle brings a distinct level of honor. I know a man in Haiti who carries a strong mantle in his life; presidents would come to see him as though he was the president. Think about the honor of Billy Graham, Pastor Benny Hinn, Apostle Guillermo Maldonado, Bishop David Oyedepo. I would venture to say that men like this, and many others, carry a level of divine honor that even wealthier men don't have. A true individual with a mantle has, in some cases, more honor than even powerful politicians. Nobody elects a man of God. His honor comes directly from his mantle. We still talk about Moses, Elijah, and Samuel today. Honor is released on your name. You are held in high esteem. You need this to be effective in ministry, and that's why Satan works so fervently and tirelessly to bring dishonor to servants of God with a mantle. A mantle replaces marketing, self-promotion, and branding, because heaven has deemed you worthy in the Lord to be held in high renown. Due to the nature of a mantle, it attracts tremendous jealousy that you must be prepared for. David had to deal with the wrath and fury of Saul's jealousy after the women of Israel were celebrating David as second to none.

Robe

A mantle is defined as a robe. A robe speaks of royalty. It's a symbol of kingdom authority. People who carry a mantle walk in tremendous authority. They can bring solutions to society that politicians just absolutely cannot. It's divine authority that can solve the divisive issues of our time, worldwide. Only Moses could quiet the cry of the children of Israel in their captivity in Egypt. A mantle is a sign of heavenly royalty. In a society, there are not many individuals who are considered royalty. Who instructed the wise men to lay frankincense, gold, and myrrh before the King of Israel, Jesus? There's a reason why Moses and Elijah were called lords.

Splendor

If you do a word study on the term "mantle," you will see that it also means "splendor." One of the definitions of "splendor" is impressiveness. Moses' ability by the Lord to perform signs and wonders even caused the magicians to be impressed and to say, "This is truly the finger of God." Think about how amazed many were when Jesus came on the scene—many people would say, "Who is this man?" Nicodemus was impressed with Jesus, saying, "No one can do such miracles, unless God was with Him." The children of Israel would look in awe at Moses as the glory of God rested upon him. A man or woman with a mantle is impressive. To impress is to affect deeply, or strongly, in mind or heart. A man with a mantle will turn an adulterous Samaritan woman into an evangelist. When the Queen of Sheba saw what God did with Solomon, in the first ten verses of 1 Kings, chapter 10, she lost her breath. She was deeply and strongly affected by the wisdom and prosperity of Solomon. God has millions of ways to impress humanity through humanity, and it's called a mantle.

Cloak made of fur or fine material

Simply put: for a garment of fur to be produced, an animal must die. There were mantles made of fur. The price was the death of animals. Other mantles were made of various fine materials that had an expensive cost. A true mantle requires an individual to pay a price. It doesn't come cheap. It can cost your deeply-rooted plans in life. It can also cost friends and meaningful relationships. When God is elevating you, it will change the context of many relationships. The mantle will interrupt your life, your family, your pleasure, and your dreams. Something in your life must die. This is what's not being taught today in our "feel-good Christianity." Everything is easy, and nothing comes with a price.

Prophet's garment

I don't believe a mantle can be limited to just a prophet's ministry today, but a mantle is mainly prophetic. Not all prophets are on the same level. With today's prophet-happy culture, where everybody is a prophet, there is a necessity for prophets to arise and walk in their mantle. There are many prophets who go by the name doctor or pastor who are really prophets. Due to the lack of honor and recognition of the prophetic office, it has forced true prophets to elevate the title of pastor. Yet, without naming names, I am convinced that many men of God who are well-respected are prophets, and that should give those called to this ministry peace. I truly believe that the office of a mantled prophet is not a title, but a garment. It should be seen more than anything. We need major prophets today who walk in a heavy mantle to bring order, structure, and decency to the prophetic office. This was the ministry of Samuel. He had what was called a school of prophets or company of prophets. This book is truly a clarion call to order in the prophetic through major prophets. A prophet who has a passed-on mantle is on another level. He's a prophetic leader of prophetic leaders.

Magnificence

Magnificence speaks of beauty! "Beauty" is defined as something that brings pleasure to the senses. A mantle brings spiritual pleasure to the spiritual senses. Think about how spiritually beautiful a sight it was to see Moses part the Red Sea, Joshua still the sun, Elijah call down fire from heaven, Elisha turn empty vessels into vessels of oil for the debt cancellation of a prophet's widow, and of course, the beautiful miracles that Jesus did. It's beautiful to see! What God wants to do in your life will be a sight to see. You must understand that God uses the foolish things of this world to confound the wise. He took a shepherd boy and turned him into King David. He took Joseph from a place of captivity to royalty, and it was beautiful. When speaking of the anointing upon Jesus, the prophet Isaiah writes in Isaiah 61:3 (NKJV), "To console those who mourn in Zion, to give them beauty for ashes." You will see that some of the greatest men and women of God came from ashes, and God released a mantle upon them that elevated them to a beautiful place. A mantle beautifies your life and causes areas of your life to be magnificent for human eyes to see.

The process of the mantle

The main biblical character that the Lord laid upon my spirit to draw prophetic secrets from for this book is Joshua. It could not be any more difficult than to replace Moses. Moses is mysteriously great. This man had the most unusual, intimate relationship with God. He would speak to God face to face; he would reason with God and speak to God as a man speaks to his friend. God honored Moses so much that it says in Deuteronomy 34 that to this day, nobody knows where his grave is. He lived up to 120 years old, and his eyes did not grow dim; nor, as the Bible says, was his natural vigor diminished. How do you replace a man like that? Yet, as supernatural a ministry as Moses had, Joshua's ministry was just as supernatural. Joshua commanded the sun and the moon to stand still, and they obeyed. Joshua led Israel to more supernatural military victories than Moses. The victory over Jericho is as supernatural as it comes, and Moses did not have that testimony. Joshua accomplished what Moses could not, and that was to possess the Promised Land. Yet, it was a process! Make no mistake, Joshua did not earn this status of elevation; he inherited it by receiving the supernatural mantle of Moses. You need a Moses in your life who can pass on to you, as an inheritance, the impartation needed for your elevation from God. It begins with the mantle upon another man's life—a distinct anointing of the Holy Spirit upon a person that only that individual operates in. Two people cannot operate on the earth with the same mantle. One must go. The Holy Spirit showed this to me by illustrating to me Moses, Elisha, and Jesus. All three of them had to leave the earth for their mantle or anointing to be passed on.

This is where the process is so difficult for many. As mentioned before, Joshua could not receive Moses' mantle until Moses died. Elijah had to be caught up into heaven before Elisha received a double portion. Finally, the church could not be birthed until Jesus, like Elijah, was caught up and ascended up to heaven. Therefore, the process of true elevation can take a long time. You could be serving certain men for a while. Sometimes the process of elevation is not as peaceful and functional as with Moses and Joshua; sometimes it's as divisive as Saul and David, and God is taking you through a more difficult route to elevation. No matter the card you've been dealt, you must endure the process in totality to experience the full elevation God has for you. There's no way around it. The first step to elevation is receiving a supernatural mantle. You must serve another mantled individual. I cannot stress enough how important this is. Joshua was operating under the promises of Moses. What God intended to give to Moses was given to Joshua. Joshua didn't have to earn it, or work for it—all he had to do was do certain things to position himself to receive the spirit and promises of Moses. Below, I will outline step by step the process of Joshua inheriting and receiving his supernatural mantle.

Joshua was Moses' minister

Most of the time in the Old Testament, Joshua was mentioned

as Joshua, the minister of Moses. This is so crucial to your development. Our generation has failed in this area. With the advent of social media, we are one keyboard experience away from self-exaltation and elevation. It takes nothing to make a ministry website, make a business card, brand yourself, and become Joshua without serving Moses. Yet, God has not changed His laws of elevation in the kingdom of God. Joshua was the servant of Moses; the Bible even records that Joshua called Moses "lord." Young man or woman of God, whom are you serving? Whom are you ministering to? Or are you too proud to humble yourself under a mantle's anointing? The word "minister" speaks of, in the Hebrew, serving in menial tasks. Let me break this down for you: "menial" means not requiring much skill, or lacking prestige. You are disqualified from walking in a mantle until you have served another mantle in menial tasks. For Elisha, it was washing the hands of Elijah before he would eat. That means holding that mantled man or woman of God's Bible, getting them water, driving them around, buying them food, doing the dirty work for them, making calls for them, and all the other tasks that make their life easier that are not prestigious. It's during this time that your character is formed, your integrity is birthed, and most of all, your heart is made right. You begin to develop a love, honor, and respect for the things of God. All of these self-proclaimed superstar, overnight ministers need to sit down! Therefore, there are not mighty deeds in this generation; because everybody wants to be an overnight Moses without going through a time as Joshua the minister. Joshua did Moses' dirty work. While Moses had his hands lifted in Exodus 17, Joshua was fighting in the valley against the Amalekites. It was Joshua and eleven other leaders who risked their lives to go into the Promised Land to spy it out, just to serve the assignment of Moses. Are you willing to be the servant to another powerful man or woman of God? Your life and ministry will always be limited until you obey this principle. There are people who had the chance to serve another man or woman of God with a mantle and failed because of pride and ego—and it might be time to repent and humble yourself and get back into position. Joshua followed Moses everywhere as his minister, and it brought great rewards. On the other side of your service are great rewards you cannot even imagine, and they can be summed up in one word: elevation.

The body of Christ has become out of order and an enemy of the principles of God in this area. Your effect is limited when you are unwilling to be a minister for a great man of God. This is not to say that every man or woman that comes into your life is a Moses to minister to. The key is to find a person who has a genuine mantle that you can serve. Now understand this: Joshua was not a low-level, incapable man of God. Joshua, before he was elevated, was gifted, strong, influential, and anointed. In spite of this, even though he could have left Moses and started his own army, he stuck with Moses—which I will talk about later. Just because you have success does not mean your days of serving another Moses in menial tasks are over. What I'm about to say in the next chapter will challenge you tremendously and will be an eye-opener.

One misconception that we have about the "Joshua generation" is that it represents a young generation. That's not biblical! We know, according to Joshua 24:29 (NKJV), "Now it came to pass after these things that Joshua the son of Nun, the servant of the LORD, died, being one hundred and ten years old." According to my studies of the chronological timeline of Israel, theologians say that Joshua and the children of Israel lived fifty years in the Promised Land. That would have made Joshua at least sixty years old when he entered the Promised Land, to actually have his own elevation from God to war against the enemies in the land. We know that the children of Israel in Moses' generation wandered in the wilderness for forty years before they died, so that would have made Joshua at least twenty years old when he started serving Moses. Why am I bringing this up? Not to say that you must wait this long before you are walking in your calling, but to point out that the Joshua generation does not mean a young generation. It means a new generation. It is not too late for you. It doesn't matter how old you are; you can be a part of this new generation, if you have the heart to serve a Moses. Believe it or not, the apostle Paul did not become a great apostle overnight. Actually, if you study his life, you will find that Paul was actually assisting Barnabas for years before he experienced his own elevation. Timothy served Paul faithfully; Paul called Timothy "son" and would give him menial tasks to do, like getting his garments and notebooks in 2 Timothy 4:13 (NKJV). "Bring the cloak that I left with Carpus at Troas when you come—and the books, especially the parchments." I am convinced that the only reason it took Peter just three years to become who he was is because he walked with Jesus Himself. Your elevation must be preceded by proper service to another man or woman of God.

Joshua was chosen by Moses

Here is a powerful truth. Numbers 11:28, in the American Standard Version, gives an interesting translation of who Joshua was. It says, "And Joshua the son of Nun, the minister of Moses, one of his chosen men, answered and said, My lord Moses, forbid them." Moses handpicked Joshua to be his go-to man for war and for important projects, and even allowed Joshua to be there when he would speak to God face to face. He would have never reached this second stage of his preparation for elevation if he had never served Moses. Joshua would never have recognized all of his abilities if he had never served. Listen, this is so important. Your access to the presence of a great mantle is service. David would never have had the opportunity to be recognized if he was not willing to serve Saul by refreshing him with the harp. One of the more immature statements, when you are just getting into your calling and development and trying to reach your elevation, is to say, "I can't do that, because it's not my gifting or calling." You will put your elevation in a cage before even your first stage of elevation. As a young man, Joshua didn't care what Moses asked him to do—he just wanted to be around his mantle.

I spent seven years directly and indirectly serving a great man of God, Pastor Mark David Boykin, senior pastor of Church of All Nations. Church of All Nations is a great church of over 3,000 members and has over fifty nations represented in the church. It's a Pentecostal powerhouse of a church: full time staff, organized leadership, and functional departments that are a rich training ground for ministry. I have served in almost every department in this church in some type of capacity. From the accredited Bible school—first as a three-year graduate, then a co-associate director, where I taught complex, challenging theological courses many times to students twice my age—to even participating in the Christmas productions as an old-time preacher. I've served in the Haitian ministry, where I've done everything from preaching, to typing songs for the overhead projector before services, to being chosen by my pastor to organize a national prayer movement in Haiti in front of the Haitian White House, to preaching in Haiti to over 16,000 people at the largest church on that island. I've cleaned bathrooms, done heavy lifting, done hospital visitations, answered phone calls, done all types of administrative work, and bought lunch for staff members. Listen, if it wasn't for me serving my pastor selflessly, I would not have met my wife. I was asked by my pastor to go on his behalf to represent the church and to replace him on a preaching engagement at another local church. In turn, this was the exact same church where I met the pastor who invited me to preach at his church in New York, where I ended up meeting my wife. I would not have a traveling preaching ministry if it wasn't for my association with Pastor Boykin. I've preached all over the east coast of the USA, I've preached internationally in Haiti, the Dominican Republic, the Bahamas, and have trips planned to Africa to preach at big gatherings. Yet, all this resulted from serving a mantle. This is a principle I've lived by, and I can testify that if you work the principles of the kingdom of God, you are guaranteed results.

Joshua was loyal to Moses

Loyalty in this generation is almost as scarce as an endangered animal. Contrary to belief, it's biblical, and a key revelation that you need for your elevation. It's recorded in Numbers chapter 11 that the children of Israel were complaining about a lack of meat to eat. God was so angry that He declared that for thirty days He would send so much supernatural meat that it would come out of their noses. Moses became overwhelmed with the responsibility that was upon his shoulders with the children of Israel, because every day he was the only one who had to deal with the burden of their complaints. The Lord spoke to Moses that He would take a portion of the Spirit that was upon him and place it upon seventy elders so they could bear the burden with him, and of course, Joshua was one of the elders. There were two elders, Eldad and Medad, who did not come to the ceremony; yet the spirit of Moses still came upon them, and they began to prophesy. Of course, prophecy usually draws attention, and word came back to Moses, and Joshua overheard. Therefore, Joshua demanded Moses to forbid them from prophesying. Moses' response was, "Are you jealous for my sake? Would that all the LORD's people were prophets and that the LORD would put His Spirit upon them" (Numbers 11:29 AMP). Now, that word "jealous" that Moses used is translated as zeal. Joshua was so loyal to Moses that he didn't even want someone to flow like him prophetically without following the clear instructions he gave to come to the tabernacle to be anointed. Joshua was passionate for his leader, Moses. Whoever you are passionate for is most likely your Moses. Whatever man or woman of God that you take to heart, and take personally whatever is done to them, is the mantle and anointing you are to serve. You are to stay loyal to that person.

To understand the loyalty that Joshua had for Moses exposes our generation. Today, we treat men and women of God as if they're a Chinese food buffet, where we can taste and move on from them whenever we want to; but when God assigns you to someone, it's important to be like Joshua and be zealously loyal to that person. When Moses, in Numbers 12, married a woman against the law, it's interesting that as close as Joshua was to Moses, he was nowhere to be found. Only Miriam and Aaron challenged Moses' authority by saying that he was not the only person who prophesied. Joshua was not even there, because he was too loyal to Moses to challenge him, even if he was wrong. We have lost this in our generation. Loyalty is a condition of your heart. It shows God that you are ready for the elevation He has for your life. Will you obey God, even when it hurts? Will you quit when things go wrong? How committed are you, even when there is injustice? If the Lord has placed a Moses into your life and you have not been loyal to him or her, put this book down now, and repent before the Lord and get reconnected to that mantle.

If another man of God in the camp of Israel wanted to start a Red Sea Parting Ministry and said to Joshua, "Leave Moses so you can have more honor and opportunity with me," what do you think Joshua would say? Heaven is keeping a record of your consistency in these kingdom principles, and your elevation depends upon it.

You know, you are called to be a minister to someone's mantle in a couple of ways. First, you take what happens to them personally. Even if you don't know them personally, you always feel personally affected by their challenges. Also, you will stand up to others on their behalf. It might encourage fights and quarrels, but you will defend that person. It will come naturally to you. In casual conversation, or even in pressure-filled meetings, you will not allow anyone to misrepresent your Moses. Is there any anointed servant of God that you feel like this for? If so, it's time to become that person's Joshua, because there's a mantle and anointing that God wants to release on your life.

Joshua sacrificed himself for Moses' assignment

Do you want a mantle in your life? How badly do you want it? Joshua is recorded to have made many sacrifices for Moses' assignment and got his hands dirty for his mantle many times. Actually, the first time we see Joshua in Scripture, he is fighting for Moses in Exodus chapter 17. Moses had his arms lifted by Aaron and Hur, but it was Joshua putting his neck out on the front line to fight. Think about how risky it must have been, in Numbers 12, to go spy out the Promised Land at the command of Moses. What if the spies were caught? Sacrifice is the only way to receive a mantle on your life. When a Moses has you as their minister, you will be required to sacrifice yourself for their success. A lot of times, you will not even get the credit. All of this is positioning you for your mantle. You will gain the trust of your Moses—but most importantly, God will trust you with His work, because the ministry is not about you; it's bigger than you, and you've proven your agreement by your sacrifice. Our generation doesn't want to sacrifice anything for their elevation to come. Even to go to Bible school or to serve under another man of woman of God is beneath them, and they wonder why their ministry is at a standstill. If you really are on fire to receive a freshly-anointed mantle from heaven for your assignment, find another mantled Moses and sacrifice for their assignment. Get work done for them, become their assistant, make calls for them, and sacrifice all that you can to further them, and you will position yourself to receive elevation from God.

Numbers 27:18-23 (KJV) says the following: "And the LORD said unto Moses, Take thee Joshua the son of Nun, a man in whom is the spirit, and lay thine hand upon him; and set him before Eleazar the priest, and before all the congregation; and give him a charge in their sight. And thou shalt put some of thine honour upon him, that all the congregation of the children of Israel may be obedient. And he shall stand before Eleazar the priest, who shall ask counsel for him after the judgment of Urim before the LORD: at his word shall they go out, and at his word they shall come in, both he, and all the children of Israel with him, even all the congregation. And Moses did as the LORD commanded him: and he took Joshua, and set him before Eleazar the priest, and before all the congregation: and he laid his hands upon him, and gave him a charge, as the LORD commanded by the hand of Moses." Finally, all the service and sacrifices of Joshua paid off. I want to stop right now and encourage you in the Lord. Your hard work behind the scenes in ministry is going to pay off publicly, in Jesus' name. God is not unjust to forget your labor of love. Many of you reading right now have been discouraged, because you feel like you serve and it doesn't pay off. God is getting ready to elevate you publicly. Moses prepared Joshua's elevation for him. A sign that you are elevating yourself is when there is no greater and more anointed man or woman of God than yourself, who prepared the people to receive you for the ministry. Jesus had John the Baptist crying out in the wilderness, preparing the way of the Lord. How was it that all the congregation of Israel followed Joshua's leadership so sacrificially? It's because Moses prepared the people to receive him. This is when elevation becomes smooth, and your platform becomes easy. God doesn't want you struggling to have influence. This is when nations and cities are prepared for your ministry. A mantle is not earned, it's inherited. You don't have to fight for a level that someone else has already mastered; you just get into proper position to receive it and walk right into it.

What are the signs that God has given you a spiritual father?

Supernatural divine connection

The first sign that God has given you a mantled leader, a Moses, a spiritual father, is that God supernaturally connects you two together. God, not you, must birth it. God must speak and sovereignly cause you two to cross paths. Did you manufacture it, or did God create it? Let God birth you as a son, and not yourself. Paul could not have planned to meet or cross paths with Timothy on his own volition. Paul was on his first apostolic journey in Lystra and Derbe, and the Lord connected him to Timothy. Elijah heard God say, "Anoint Elisha as prophet in your place." This is not manufactured or coerced; it is God's supernatural, divine connection.

Does that individual have a higher anointing in the area of your calling and gifting?

This is crucial. You don't have a Moses in your life so that you can just enjoy going to the movies and joking around a lot. It's not about just eating food and talking about insignificant matters. It's about you receiving a mantle, a spiritual anointing of the Holy Spirit that will bring you higher through sonship. Your association, covenant, and family loyalty together are recognized in heaven as being worthy of a transfer. Let's put personal feelings aside—does that individual have a mantle that will bring you to your destiny?

You're getting ready to receive a mantle

There is a generation of men and women who are hungry for their next level in the kingdom and are sold out for it at any cost, and I believe you are a part of that remnant. Has your heart been burning as you've been reading the pages of this book so far? Are you gifted, are you called, are you passionate and effective in what you do best? Guess what? You still need a mantle. Miracles must be a major part of your ministry, in Jesus' name. Your name is destined to be great, and this chapter is the first prophetic secret to your elevation. The Promised Land is not heaven—it's a process of elevation! Your family and your seed for generations beyond must honor your life and the great exploits of your life. Honor shall be your legacy. It all begins with prayer. Some of you may start crying as you pray this prayer out loud. You may look nothing like the elevation that God has destined for you, based on the way you picture in yourself in your mind, but I'm here to tell you that you are a Joshua in the making, and you will be elevated publicly, and all shall see the magnificence of your greatness in the kingdom. This may be the most important prayer you will pray in this season of your life. Kneel and cry out this prayer to God, and get ready for your life to change:

Father, in the name of Jesus, send me a Moses for me to serve, and to become the minister of _____. I'm ready for whatever price You will for me to pay. I will not exalt myself, but will endure the process. I will be loyal to another person's mantle before I walk in mine. Give me the heart, mind, and spirit of Joshua, that only You would elevate me. I declare in the name of Jesus, in Your timing, that after I have gone through Joshua's process in Your kingdom publicly, You will prepare my elevation with the people You've called me to lead.

In Jesus' name, Amen.

Chapter 2

EXPERIENCING TRUE
SUPERNATURAL MANIFESTATION

The word "manifestation" is defined as: "to make visible or known what has been hidden or unknown, whether by words, deeds or any other way." This is powerful, because this is the desire of every person who is hungry for God. Your desire should be that all the gifts and callings of God that are in you be made manifest in the lives of other men and women, publicly. Essentially, that is ministry. All that is locked in you to be unleashed is vital to your elevation. Before Joshua could enter the Promised Land, which represents a promise of elevation, he needed all the gifts and spiritual abilities in him to be supernaturally manifested. How else could he lead Israel to defeat Jericho, hear God prophetically against Ai, and still the sun against his enemies? These supernatural abilities were already in Joshua; he just needed Moses to get it out of him. It's one thing to be called as a prophet, and it's another thing for that calling to be made manifest in the lives of others—where you are revealing accurate, secret information about other people's lives so they must believe that God sent you as His prophet. Many of you who will be reading this chapter will begin to feel the presence of God like fire. Recently, whenever I've ministered to people on certain revelatory topics, people have begun to feel fire on their body. One of the callings on my life is to dig deep into the reservoir of people's lives and prophetically bring out of them who they are in Christ. Lately, I had this experience with my wife, Prophetess Naomi Louis. We were having a normal conversation, and the Holy Spirit fell on our phone call, and I began to prophetically make manifest her calling—and it was like connecting the dots for her, and since then her life has never been the same. Before you even continue reading this chapter, I'm going to ask you with all your heart to repeat a prayer below, for you to receive revelation of who you are called to be and what you're gifted to do. It must be made manifest. Many of you reading this book don't know what God has called or gifted you to do, and I prophesy in Jesus' name that you are getting ready to receive that revelation, in Jesus' name. Many of you know your gift, but it's dormant or inactive—and as you read this chapter, everything inactive or sleeping inside of you is getting ready to awaken, in Jesus' name. First, pray this prayer below:

Father, in the name of Jesus,

I believe You have called me and have gifted me for Your purpose in my life. I humbly ask that You would impart into my life a spirit of courage, that all that's asleep in me would supernaturally be made manifest and awaken, that I may accomplish Your purpose in my life. As You did for Joshua, I declare in faith that I believe You will do for me.

In Jesus' name,

Amen.

For this chapter, we will be focusing on chapter one of the book of Joshua and correlating it with New Testament revelation. First, let's understand the stage of Joshua's life when the Lord audibly spoke to him. For forty years Joshua had been serving a man named Moses, whom he saw do bigger-than-life miracles. When he was in his late teen years, he personally experienced the miraculous ministry of Moses by seeing the ten signs and wonders that Moses did against Pharaoh in Egypt—and in an instant, went from being a slave in Egypt to a free citizen of Israel. It had such a profound effect on his life that he decided to find a way to serve this great man of God. As Moses was delivering the law to God's people and leading them through the wilderness, he noticed this young man's willingness to always honor and serve the mantle on his life. Maybe Joshua would bring food to Moses, or possibly Moses could just see the spirit and heart of this young man. I can just see Joshua now, praying in his tent, "Lord, please use me like You used Moses; I want to be near him and to be his minister." We don't know for sure, but something inside of Joshua sparked a strong desire to serve Moses. Being the prophet that Moses was, he identified the warrior in Joshua even though Israel had never been involved in a war before, so it must have been God who revealed this to Moses. The first time that we see Joshua, in Exodus chapter 17, we see him fighting against the Amalekites in the valley of Rephidim. Joshua loved Moses so much that he was willing to put his life on the line to fight for him—but in that moment, it served as a revelation to him and to Moses that this young man named Joshua was gifted to battle.

Your gifts and calling must be pulled out of you by someone else. God raises up men and women of God who will, under their leadership and mentorship, bring to the surface who you are. It was Moses who helped Joshua understand his potential to fight. He helped him in his gifting and calling in warfare by lifting his hands on the top of the hill to ensure that Joshua would supernaturally have the victory over God's enemies. Why is this important? Everyone needs a Moses to lift their rod on the top of the hill to help them discover the potential inside of them. Do you remember Matthew chapter 10? Jesus, just like Moses, chooses seventy men and gives them His power and commands them, in verses seven and eight, "And as you go, preach, saying, 'The kingdom of heaven is at hand.' Heal the sick, cleanse the lepers, raise the dead, cast out demons. Freely you have received, freely give" (NKJV). Just like Moses did for Joshua and the seventy elders in total, so did Jesus in verse 5 send forth and command His disciples. In this moment, before they birthed the church on their own, it was important that what was in them would begin to be made manifest. Now here is a principle: your gifts will always be made manifest openly before your calling. Your calling is simply God's divine, supernatural invitation to you to fulfill His specific purpose for you on earth. Your gifts are what He equips you with to accomplish it. If your calling is to win the lost to Jesus worldwide by preaching and healing the sick, don't you think God will gift you to preach and operate in gifts of healing? Your gifts compliment the call. Yet, we have an epidemic in the body of Christ where many men and women, young and old, simply do not know what they're either gifted or called to do—and it's causing great frustration and discouragement, even in many of you who are reading this book. What is the solution? Below, let's walk through a few simple, prophetic keys to experiencing true supernatural manifestation of your gifts and calling.

You need to connect to an apostolic or prophetic mantle

I understand that this is going to be a very controversial part of the book, but I'm ready to go there if you are. Satan has done a very good job of deceiving the church about the ministry of the apostle and prophet. There are mainline, Pentecostal denominations today who have included in their constitution and bylaws that they will not address these offices at all. There are many preachers who take the pulpit and say day and night that everybody wants to be an apostle and prophet, and are coming hard at young men and women who are called to those offices. Yet, let's go deep on a couple of truths and realities of the leadership today.

The fault lies with the leadership of today

We can agree that Jesus is the same yesterday, today, and forevermore. In the book of Revelation, Jesus addressed seven churches in Ephesus, Smyrna, Pergamos, Thyatira, Sardis,

Philadelphia, and Laodicea. In each of the churches there were all types of abuses among the congregation. One of the biggest problems was in the church of Thyatira. There was a woman who was calling herself a prophetess and even teaching the church members that it was okay to fornicate. In contrast, what is profound and a wakeup call is that Jesus did not confront the abuse of the Jezebel as a church member, but He confronted the senior pastor, the angel of the church. Actually, Jesus only addressed sharply with a rebuke the leaders of those churches. If there is abuse in the church today, it's the fault of the leadership.

Here's a reality: there's a huge difference between an overly zealous, misguided individual and a false prophet or apostle. We throw around the title "false" to everybody. Remember the prophets of Baal and Ashtoreth, who were working for the queen, were false prophets doing witchcraft. The sorcerer whom Paul declared blindness on for a season was a false prophet. To call someone a false minister is to say that they are working directly for Satan. Many of these so-called false prophets and apostles are just misguided up-and-coming leaders who are overzealous and have not ever had a legitimate leader to lead them without being insecure, jealous, in competition with them—or even worse, attacking them in destructive ways. I have news for these types of leaders: your mediocrity is not someone else's emergency. There are up-and-coming leaders who have been hurt and crushed by leaders who were supposed to raise them up and show them which way they should go. Some young ministers' only crime is being gifted and anointed without true, competent guidance. The average leader of a church today does not spend more than five minutes with God in prayer nor in the Word. So, here comes someone in your church who is on fire, and you are intimidated and threatened by them because you are not at the God-ordained level you should be. Truth be told, many leaders of churches today, like

Saul, have been rejected by God and don't even know it; they are attacking young up-and-coming Davids in their church, and throwing spears at them, and causing a generation to live in caves. Many of you reading this book are currently a victim of this, or have been a victim of this. You have trust issues, and you feel like you cannot trust anyone to be your Moses. As you read this book, may supernatural healing and restoration touch your heart, in Jesus' name.

The answer to someone who may be zealous without knowledge in the timing and function of their calling is not to destroy them with your words. There was a story my wife told me about a young man in her church when she was growing up that everybody made fun of because he was acting like he was a pastor, and everyone would call him a "wannabe pastor." The church ended up shutting down the youth group. Years later, my wife told me that some of the young men from the youth group are either in jail or are completely away from God and suffering the consequences of it in their personal life. Yet, this young man who was called the "wannabe pastor" has his own flourishing church with a beautiful family today. I would rather, as a leader, deal with someone who's prematurely longing to walk in the ministry of an apostle or prophet than see these same young leaders walk away from God, either on their way to hell or living in hell on earth. This generation needs a Moses in their lives, not rejection.

Back to our original point, you need someone to manifest what's hidden inside of you. Joshua experienced a fresh, supernatural manifestation of what was inside of him through the life of Moses. There are many supernatural, unseen walls of resistance that suppress what's inside of you. You feel the fire inside of you, but it can't manifest itself. Remember, the word "manifest" means to make visible or known what has been hidden or unknown, whether by words, deeds, or any other way. You have a word in you, but it's hidden. You have a song in you, but it's unknown how to get it out. You have the hunger to move in the supernatural, and it consumes you, but it's locked inside of you, and you need an apostle or prophet to get it out of you. David went from being a shepherd to a king because a prophet laid oil upon him. Who was Elisha before Elijah threw his mantle upon him? We must break down these walls once and for all, for all that is in you to come out. Below, we are going to attack head-on what the Holy Spirit revealed to me that holds back this generation from experiencing a supernatural manifestation of all that's in them.

Receiving impartation from the wrong person

It says in Numbers 27:18 (NKJV), "And the Lord said to Moses: 'Take Joshua the son of Nun with you, a man in whom is the Spirit, and lay your hand on him.'" This is very profound. Joshua already had something deposited in him from God, just like you do. Yet, God still found it necessary for Moses, by the leading of God, to lay hands on him. As we will cover later, when God replaced Moses with Joshua, one of the profound, prophetic statements from God was, "As I was with Moses, so I will be with you." So, that means the spiritual level and divine connection of Moses with God was imparted into Joshua, which was the reason for his success.

Well, the opposite is just as true. Having the wrong spiritual leader impart into your life will be the reason for the lack of manifestation of what's in you, and the cause of your failure. What's an impartation? It simply means to give or share spiritually what's in you. To open your spirit to someone as they lay hands upon you is serious business. There are many ways to impart into others.

Laying on of hands

The hands of an individual are a divine channel for impartation. Jesus effortlessly touched the mother-in-law of Peter, who was sick, and instantly she was healed. Ananias laid hands on Paul's eyes, and he was instantly healed after he was blinded by a one-on-one encounter with Jesus. Isaac laid hands on Jacob, and a blessing was transferred upon Jacob—even though he deceived his father, Isaac. When God would use His prophets, the Bible would say that the hand of the Lord was upon them. God has chosen hands to be the spiritual channel for spiritual transfers to take place; when the wrong hands are laid upon you, it can damage your life. To have the wrong person lay hands on you for ministry and your assignment can hinder you from reaching your promised land of elevation. If God is not with someone, and that same individual shares what's in him or her in you, then guess what will be your result?

Teaching

Teaching releases an impartation in your life. There is a spirit behind every teaching. Paul spoke about doctrines of demons. In turn, these were doctrines that were being taught by men with a demonic spirit behind them, which entered people's lives. There are some people who have exposed themselves to the wrong teaching, and it takes years to recover from the effects of those false impartations. Here is a principle that I teach and preach everywhere I go: you can cast out a demon, but you can't cast out a mentality. Teaching imparts a mentality that has permanent effects. Some of the most demonic cults, and even political movements, were satanic impartations through certain taught philosophies. Look at terrorists today: they are teaching young men and women to commit gruesome acts of murder in the name of religion, through false teaching. The right teaching will shift you into your promised land of elevation.

Through the doctrinal teachings of the apostle Paul in his epistles, he was able to impart apostolic power in the churches that he either planted himself, or churches that he oversaw. There is a spiritual transfer that occurs once words in and of themselves are released into the atmosphere, depending on the intention of the person's heart who spoke those words. That's why Jesus said, "Out of the abundance of the heart, the mouth speaks." It is very possible that someone can hinder your elevation out of the words that they speak. Who is teaching you and transferring spiritual deposits to you through their messages, books, and even videos?

Music

When Saul the king needed deliverance from a distressing spirit, he called upon David to play his harp, because through the music that echoed from the harp there was a vicarious impartation that he received that liberated him. Elisha asked for an anointed musician to impart and stir the prophetic in him to prophesy the word of the Lord to a king. In the Haitian background where I come from, voodoo is a very influential, false religion which is very much inspired by music. Let me just say this: if you are a praise and worship leader and you also sing in a secular band that plays in demonic, worldly environments like night clubs, then you are hindering the manifestation of God's full arsenal of power inside of you when you minister at your church, because you are releasing a false anointing upon the people. Music is a powerful vehicle for spiritual impartation. This is so because the global music industry is worth $15 billion, and it has gone down from its earlier-decade worth of $20 billion. Ask God what worship music to listen to. Don't just listen to anything. Every praise and worship song has a sound, and you must find your sound to trigger manifestation to take place inside of you.

Relationships

Remember, bad company corrupts good character. Why? It's because the real you is your spirit. If you are connected to a certain spirit of a man too long, it will either catapult or corrupt you. A little leaven leavens the whole lump. The Bible says, "Guard your heart with all diligence, for out of it flow the issues of life." Everyone has issues, and those issues can be spiritually imparted to you. There's a reason why most of the time, we saw Joshua with either Moses or Caleb. That is wisdom. Ask the Holy Spirit whose issues have been spiritually holding you back.

Your delay in your journey to the promised land of elevation may be due to who is imparting in your life. Some people are in wrong churches which are delaying the supernatural manifestation of their gifts and callings to take place. The right church can bring to the surface all that is in you, yet the wrong church can suppress all that's in you. Here is a revelation that the Holy Spirit spoke to me: just because someone is your pastor doesn't make them your mantle or Moses. Some of you may be attending a church where your assignment may be to be a giver and not a receiver. Your pastor loves you, but they don't have the mantle you need to experience the supernatural manifestation of what's inside of you. Ask the Holy Spirit who is the Moses that you are zealous for what's on them, that you are to be loyal to, and you will inherit that supernatural anointing that's upon their life.

It may even be someone you do not know personally. These principles don't only work for individuals that you know personally. There are men and women of God out there that you may never have the opportunity to meet personally, but the Lord desires the anointing that is on them to fall on you. If this is you, then you would ask, how can I receive and get an impartation from them? The answer is easy! Buy their books, spiritually watch and feed yourself from intently watching their videos, be zealous for what's on them, attend their events as much as you can, and God will honor your willingness. Pastor Benny Hinn never had a personal relationship with Kathryn

Kuhlman, but to this day he talks about this mighty general of God, and how a double portion of her anointing truly rests upon him after he attended one of her large gatherings. The Lord is showing me that by whatever means necessary, He must release a mantle and anointing on your life—even if it's through unconventional means, He will do it. It doesn't matter how dysfunctional your ministry situation may be right now; the Holy Spirit wants you to know that there's a transfer coming upon you. The mantle God has for you will find you at your place of faithfulness. Elisha was faithfully doing an insignificant job for his family, and here comes Elijah out of nowhere and casts his mantle on him. God is speaking to a Moses about you. There are divine connections that have already been ordained for you to receive your impartation.

Not embracing your own calling and gifting

The first thing God said to Joshua, in Joshua chapter 1, was, "Moses my servant is dead." I believe that the need for a man to die before you can operate in the transfer of the anointing imparted into you was done away with by Jesus. Moses and Elijah were types and shadows of Jesus, meaning their lives biblically were symbols of the life of Jesus to come. Moses said that God would raise up a Prophet like himself, which was Jesus. The same way that the spirit of Elijah did not fall in a double portion until Elisha saw him caught up into heaven is the same way that the Spirit of Jesus fell upon the 120 in the upper room after they saw Him caught up into the third heaven. You must embrace who you are in the Lord. This formula will bring you to the clear understanding of how a mantle is received from the Lord, because you don't want to worship anyone else but the Lord Himself. Joshua was so loyal to Moses that he would not move forward with the children of Israel until Moses died. Isn't it interesting that the prophet Isaiah never had the heavenly vision of the Lord until King Uzziah died? It reads like this in Isaiah 6:1 (NKJV): "In the year that

King Uzziah died, I saw the Lord sitting on a throne, high and lifted up, and the train of His robe filled the temple." Sometimes, the person we serve can become an idol, to the point where you never let what was is in you manifest because you are so focused on someone else.

Without you realizing it, you will neglect your gift in you—because you feel like there's no point in you using what God has given you because you can never be like the Moses you look up to. However, remember that the same God that was with Moses was with Joshua as well. As some of you are reading this, you are being set free to experience the manifestation of what's buried inside of you. Most often this is where discouragement stems from, because you can feel like God can only use that person and not you. As a result, this can become idolatry—so the image of Moses must die in your mind. God is going to use you individually like He's never used someone else, because God is with you!

Not embracing the prophetic in your life

The next revelation the Holy Spirit gave me came from Joshua chapter 1, in the very first line in verse 1, preceding the statement "it came to pass." It reads as follows: "Now after the death of Moses the servant of the Lord it came to pass, that the Lord spake unto Joshua the son of Nun, Moses' minister" (KJV). Here is a divine principle: the only path to your promised land of elevation is through a prophetic word. A prophetic word must come before your elevation comes to pass. All throughout scripture, it was the power of the prophetic word in the lives of great leaders that carried them to their elevation. Abraham received a prophetic word in Genesis 12 that is still coming to pass today. The Lord later spoke prophetically to Abraham about Isaac, which came to pass in Genesis 21, which was part of his elevation from God. Moses was prophetically visited by God and received the word of the Lord from Jehovah that

He would set the children of Israel free from Pharaoh, and that very fulfillment of prophecy carried Moses to a level of elevation that few in the history of Israel ever knew. According to Deuteronomy 34:10-12 (KJV), "And there arose not a prophet since in Israel like unto Moses, whom the Lord knew face to face, in all the signs and the wonders, which the LORD sent him to do in the land of Egypt to Pharaoh, and to all his servants, and to all his land, and in all that mighty hand, and in all the great terror which Moses shewed in the sight of all Israel." David's elevation began with a prophetic anointing ceremony administered by the prophet Samuel. Samuel prophetically anointed David as the next king of Israel at the age of sixteen, and the fulfillment of that word has caused Jesus Christ to be named "the Son of David." Jesus' life was a line-upon-line fulfillment of hundreds of messianic prophecies that came to pass, one by one, in the book of Matthew. Paul's elevation as an apostle was all due to the prophetic words that he received from Christ Himself coming to pass. It reads as follows: "At midday, O king, along the road I saw a light from heaven, brighter than the sun, shining around me and those who journeyed with me. And when we all had fallen to the ground, I heard a voice speaking to me and saying in the Hebrew language, 'Saul, Saul, why are you persecuting Me? It is hard for you to kick against the goads.' So I said, 'Who are You, Lord?' And He said, 'I am Jesus, whom you are persecuting. But rise and stand on your feet; for I have appeared to you for this purpose, to make you a minister and a witness both of the things which you have seen and of the things which I will yet reveal to you. I will deliver you from the Jewish people, as well as from the Gentiles, to whom I now I send you, to open their eyes, in order to turn them from darkness to light, and from the power of Satan to God, that they may receive forgiveness of sins and an inheritance among those who are sanctified by faith in Me'" (Acts 26:13-18 NKJV).

In essence, if you don't make room in your life to honor prophets and prophetic words that come your way, you may never arrive in your promised land of elevation. The Bible says emphatically in the latter part of 2 Chronicles 20:20 (NKJV), "Believe His prophets, and you shall prosper." Jesus said, "He who receives a prophet in the name of a prophet shall receive a prophet's reward" (Matthew 10:41 NKJV). Prophecy is a sworn verdict from heaven. God said in Isaiah 55:11 (NKJV), "So shall My word be that goes forth from My mouth; it shall not return to Me void, but it shall accomplish what I please, and it shall prosper in the thing for which I sent it." This is why the apostle Paul said, "Do not despise prophecies."

It says in Joshua 1:1 that "it came to pass." I prophesy over your life that your elevation is getting ready to come to pass, in the name of Jesus. Receive it!

Not moving when God says move

Here is another kingdom principle that is imperative for your elevation: obedience is not a desire, but an action. The Lord prophetically declared to Joshua, "Arise," meaning, "Joshua, it's time to move!" Yes, there were still uncertainties, and so many questions to answer. How are we going to possess the promised land of elevation when the Jordan River is in our way? God still is saying to you, "Arise." Well, God, if Moses could not accomplish this, how am I going to do it? God still says, "Arise." The Hebrew meaning of "arise" is to stand, perform, and accomplish. The Holy Spirit is not your Doer; He is your Helper. You must make the calls, you must raise the money, you must prepare the messages, you must prepare yourself, and you must perform the tasks. This is where many miss their elevation, when all they need in order to move forward is a word from God. It doesn't need to make sense to you. Abraham was following the voice of God, not the voice of a GPS. Moses was following a cloud by day and a pillar of fire by night—that's it. No one in the Bible had all the details and facts upfront. If it had been so, then why would we need faith? Many of you reading this book are at the stage of arising by faith. You are nervous, you feel there's not enough security, and you're in a very uncomfortable season of transition. The word of the Lord to you nonetheless is: Arise!

Not prohibiting people from stopping you from your elevation

This is a big barrier. God tells Joshua directly in Joshua 1:5 (NKJV), "No man shall be able to stand before you all the days of your life; as I was with Moses, so I will be with you. I will not leave you nor forsake you." This means that men will always be a barrier to your elevation. The devil will send Joseph's brothers, Job's friends, threats from Jezebel, seduction from Delilah, intimidation from Goliath, negativity from Sanballat, and betrayal from Judas. No matter who you are and how nice you may be to people, they will try to keep you from possessing your promised land. David, just like Jesus, had to deal with the lack of belief from his family. Yes, even family can become an obstacle. The end of Joshua 1:5 (NKJV) says, from God, "I will not leave you nor forsake you." In other words, in plain words: "Just trust Me." If people are trying to hinder your path to the promised land of elevation and you haven't even accomplished anything yet, that means you are close to your elevation. This is a barrier that God promises will not be able to stand in your path.

Not resisting the spirit of fear

Three times in the first nine verses in Joshua chapter 1, God repeatedly says to Joshua, "Be of good courage." In other words, do not be afraid. Fear is not just a feeling; it's a spirit. It comes through other people, it comes in the form of thoughts in your mind; it can be a bad dream, or a spiritual attack tangibly on your soul. Jesus, many times in the gospels, would say, "Do not fear." The Bible even says in the book of Revelation that the fearful will be in hell. Paul said that God has not given us a spirit of fear. Gideon had to tell all the fearful soldiers of his army to go home. Why? Well, here is a sobering kingdom principle: God cannot use fearful people, and will not elevate individuals with fear. It could be that you're afraid to fail, or you're afraid of the opposition, or the attention of elevation is intimidating. You must bind the spirit of fear out of your life and possess your destiny of elevation in Jesus' name. Courage is your portion in this season of your life; speak it, declare it, and prophesy it like Ezekiel over your life, in Jesus' name.

Not speaking and meditating on the prophetic word on your life

Joshua 1:8 (NKJV), "This Book of the Law shall not depart from your mouth, but you shall meditate in it day and night, that you may observe to do according to all that is written in it," many times is interpreted that in order to be successful, you must be a student of the Bible. I believe this to be true, and I also believe that this verse must be coupled with a prophetic word as well. Remember, Moses prophetically received the Law from God on Mount Sinai, beginning in Exodus 19. It was a direct word from God! God said unto Moses, "You must speak this word every chance you get, meditate on it, observe, and then will you make your ways prosperous and successful." Do you remember what David did when he was getting ready to fight Goliath? King Saul promised to make the killer of this giant the son-in-law of the king and a wealthy man, tax-free—that was the promise. Therefore, before David went to challenge Goliath, he wanted to be reminded of the promise once again. Why did he do that? The reason is because you must focus on your prophetic word when your reality looks quite the opposite. Paul told his spiritual son Timothy to war with the prophetic words that were upon his life. Many of you have lost faith in what God has spoken to you, and it's causing failure and delay. Today is your day to go back to what God said concerning you. Write it down and read it every day, pray it, declare it, discuss it with your spouse or close friend. Let it consume your life, and your barriers will be broken, in Jesus' name.

Not destroying the spirit of discouragement

Finally, in Joshua 1:9 (NKJV), God commands Joshua: "Do not be afraid, nor be dismayed, for the LORD your God is with you wherever you go." There is a reason why this is the last thing that is mentioned by God. It is because every time Satan has tried all of the above attacks against you and has failed, his last resort is to send discouragement your way. The following are eight signs of discouragement in your life, from the life of Elijah:

Isolation: When Elijah was threatened by Jezebel, he ran alone to a cave.

Fear: Even though Elijah defeated 850 false prophets, he ran away from one woman.

Fatigue: Elijah slept in the cave. Discouragement is a direct result of not resting your whole man.

Lack of self-worth: Elijah said, "I'm no better than my fathers." When you start not believing and devaluing yourself, then this is a major sign of discouragement. This even led Elijah to be suicidal. The answer is to rebuke the spirit of discouragement, in the name of Jesus.

Viewing others as better than yourself: Elijah viewed his accomplishments as being at the bottom of the list. Learn how to celebrate yourself.

Disruption of normalcy: Because Elijah was running away from Jezebel miles away, it disrupted the normalcy of his prophetic calling.

Bad perception of life: Elijah became very negative and pessimistic about his assignment as a prophet. Negativity is a sign of discouragement.

Unwilling to fight your battles: Elijah lost his fight and just ran for his life. If you are running from your challenges you are discouraged, and in the name of Jesus, BE FREE, IN JESUS' NAME!

Once these barriers are destroyed and you fully receive a fresh impartation under the mantle of a true man or woman of God, you will see all that God has placed in you manifest, or come to the surface—and the exciting news is that God is going to do it publicly, for His name to be glorified.

Chapter 3

OPERATING IN SUPERNATURAL MIGHT

One misconception about the Promised Land is that it represents heaven. Though it's an understandable interpretation and not an evil-intended conclusion, it's simply wrong! One of the many reasons why the Promised Land can't represent heaven is because there were enemies inhabiting the Promised Land that Joshua and the armies of Israel had to dispossess by killing them. Therefore, the Promised Land simply represents a promise from God of elevation. That promise could mean many things to many people. No matter what that promise is for you, a couple of things are clear. The promise: (1) is a prophecy from God; (2) is big and affects generations; (3) will not come overnight; (4) and finally, will require a long, continuous FIGHT! Now this is very crucial to your elevation, because your elevation is always revealed through a prophetic word. Let's review this in detail to understand it completely. Originally, it was prophetically promised to Abraham, not to Moses, that he would possess the Promised Land—then to Isaac, to Jacob, to Moses, and finally to Joshua. Deuteronomy 1:8 (NKJV): "See, I have set the land before you; go in and possess the land which the LORD swore to your fathers—to Abraham, Isaac, and Jacob—to give to them and their descendants after them."

Now understand this: the land was prophesied to Abraham—and then five generations later, it was possessed by Joshua! The initial obvious question is, why so long? Theologically, there is much to say about why it took so long. It can range anywhere from the predestination of God's plan for humanity, to simply God's sovereignty that we will never truly understand, to the disobedience of Moses—which could have been part of God's plan and resulted in God's permissible will, which allowed Joshua to stumble upon this assignment. It can go a lot of different ways that I don't believe we will all fully understand, but one thing is for sure—it took a long time for this word to come to pass. It was a prophecy directly from the mouth of God that did not come to pass the next day, year, decade, generation, century, or even the next couple of generations. It took five generations to come to pass. That points to just how big this promise was.

It affected an entire nation! It was a promise to one man with a mantle, but it affected an entire nation of men and women, young and old—and it is still relevant today. Therefore, the Promised Land represents more than just a car, a house, a ministry, or money; it's the promised, prophetic destiny of a people! Simply put, it's elevation. It's materialistic in the Old Testament, but has spiritual implications in this New Testament dispensation. We truly devalue this promise by saying that it's solely limited to a car or a house! Amongst many things, this promise had to do with God elevating the children of Israel as compared to other countries. Imagine: for centuries, the children of Israel were a nation with an army, but never owned their own territory. Let's think about the description of this land for a second: a place of milk and honey, where every tribe would have a piece of land. What nation on earth can boast of their own territory? The Lord wanted to elevate His people! Just like God's will is to elevate you! Deuteronomy 26:19 (NKJV): "And that he will set you high above all nations which He has made, in praise, in name, and in honor, and that you may be a holy people to the LORD your God, just as He has spoken." This is the clearest and most powerful verse to illustrate my point of God's heart to elevate His people! I prophesy to you that this is God's plan for your life! God's heart to elevate His people, according to this verse, is all throughout Scripture. How many times in the Bible does it state that He would make certain men's names great, and/or how many times would they see that reality manifest in their lives? You cannot deny the greatness of the judges in the book of Judges, or certain kings in the Bible like David, Solomon, Hezekiah, Josiah, and Jehoshaphat, to name a few. Think about the greatness of God's prophets like Elijah, Elisha, Daniel, and Samuel. Can we deny the greatness of Nehemiah, Esther, and Ezra? The apostles were men of unbelievable renown in their day because of their elevation in God's kingdom. Throughout church history, God has raised up great generals and servants of God for His glory, and I prophesy over your life that this greatness shall fall upon you, in Jesus Christ's mighty name. God wants you to resemble His power and honor as the one and only God of the universe! In your blood there is flowing the distinct prestige, honor, and greatness of God. Your life cannot be insignificant after you read this book, in the name of Jesus Christ! Yet, there is one thing we must not allow ourselves to forget: elevation does not happen by resting, worshipping, praising, or simply just by normal praying, but by fighting and spiritual warfare. Once you get near this promised land of elevation there will be new devils, principalities, territorial spirits, and ancient demons that have been enjoying themselves at the expense of your rightful possession! Joseph's brothers will throw you in a pit; Job's friends will attack you; Sanballat will attempt to weaken you; Saul will try to murder you; Haman will try to make your whole ministry extinct; sickness will happen; poverty will knock at your door; betrayal will bite you; the Pharisees will try to manipulate you; every kind of Satan's most effective demonic weapons will be launched at you—and it will be an all-out war! You don't have a choice but to fight. Until you have peace all around you, and you are experiencing God's undeniable elevation that can be seen by your place of honor, blessing, and prestige, you must be in a perpetual fight and war. This is where the mantle of Joshua was so exceptional, because he operated in supernatural might! "Might" here is speaking of his violent spiritual nature. He was a ruthless, aggressive, no-nonsense, merciless general of spiritual warfare. If he had to still the sun to kill his enemies, he did. He executed his enemies, put fear into the hearts of his foes—and though unaware, even was willing to challenge the Commander of the Army of the Lord, until it was revealed that it was God with us Himself. If this is not your nature, then you will not reach your highest levels in the kingdom. It takes spiritual violence, aggression, and ruthlessness in the Spirit against the strong demonic forces fighting against you. Some of you reading this will have to battle generational demons of witchcraft, voodoo, and all types of deliberate, intentional works of Satan, opposing you even through people. What are you going to do? Are you going to ignore the reality of the nations of enemies inhabiting your elevation, or are you going to operate in a spirit of might?

The hand of the Lord releases into you violent spiritual might

The Lord began to speak to me about what caused Joshua to be such a dangerous military general against the kings who were inhabiting the Promised Land. Yes, through the mantle of Moses, Joshua inherited the wisdom for warfare. The wisdom of the strategies that Joshua received against Jericho and Ai was just too much to handle for those kingdoms. Yet, Joshua 4:23-24 (NKJV) was a revelation I came across in my studies.

"For the LORD your God dried up the waters of the Jordan before you until you had crossed over, as the LORD your God did to the Red Sea, which He dried up before us until we had crossed over; that all the peoples of the earth may know the hand of the LORD, that it is mighty, that you may fear the LORD your God forever." What stuck out to me was the phrase "the hand of the Lord." We don't see this specific type of description of God's work in many individuals' lives in Scripture. In careful research, I discovered that the hand of the Lord has two major functions: violent warfare, and supernatural miracles. The hand of the Lord upon Joshua's life was a direct benefit of inheriting the mantle of Moses. Remember, in Joshua 1:5 (NKJV), God said, "No man shall be able to stand before you all the days of your life; as I was with Moses, so I will be with you. I will not leave you nor forsake you." There are many phenomenal books written on deliverance and spiritual warfare that would be able to break down how to destroy principalities and strongholds. I will write many books on this—but I believe it begins with the mantle from the leader. Joshua was going to face more warfare than even Moses and could not use profound warfare strategies without the anointed mantle of a great man of God like Moses.

I was speaking to a man of God, and he pointed out to me and my wife one of the benefits of sonship. It's found in Deuteronomy 1:11 (NKJV), "May the LORD God of your fathers make you a thousand times more numerous than you are, and bless you as He has promised you!" Notice two things: first, that it says "the God of your fathers." That is sonship at its finest at work in your life, when you learn from your fathers. Secondly, there is a blessing attached to being a son; you cannot *not* be blessed. As a matter of fact, there is exponential growth and expansion from the very place where you are positioned in your life as we speak. Can you imagine where you'll be or how far you will go, a thousand times more than where you are? It's impossible for you to lose, and impossible for you to fail; you will be a force to be reckoned with. I mean, everything in your life changes for the better, and not the worse, in every area of your life—spiritually, financially, physically, mentally, emotionally, and the list goes on and on, because of a thousand-fold blessing. Ladies and gentlemen, it's to your advantage and for your future generations for you to be sons, because everyone connected to you will be blessed. Beloved, you cannot reach the heights you desire in the kingdom without becoming the son or daughter of a great man or woman of God with a genuine mantle. Yes, you must know God for yourself intimately, but there is a certain level of anointing you will never see unless it's passed on to you through sonship. Also, he went further on to explain that even Jesus, being the Son of God, had a spiritual Father in heaven, as stated in John 5:19-20 (NKJV). "Then Jesus answered and said to them, 'Most assuredly, I say to you, the Son can do nothing of Himself, but what He sees the Father do; for whatever He does, the Son also does in like manner. For the Father loves the Son, and shows Him all things that He Himself does; and He will show Him greater works than these, that you may marvel.'" Moreover, he explained to me that the last words that are mentioned in the Old Testament were about the restoration of the hearts of the fathers to the sons and the sons to the fathers.

As far as I am concerned, it has been the many fathers in my years of ministry that have led me to where I am, such as great men of God like Pastor Mark David Boykin and Prophet Frank Nattiel who, in the most sensitive times of my life, have imparted into me the necessary anointing I needed to transition from season to season. The first time I received an extended prophetic word was in 2007. I will never forget it. It was the first service at Church of All Nations, and Pastor Mark Boykin was preaching a dynamic message from the life of Elijah. As we approached the altar call, Pastor Boykin began to operate in a powerful prophetic anointing, prophesying to many people in the service with intricate details. As he was approaching the end of the service he asked the congregation to give him a moment, and he took a deep breath and looked directly at me and said, "Brother Fred, come up here." Now, to understand the magnitude of this, I was in my second year of Bible school and my second year of being a believer. Church of All Nations is a very structured, orderly ministry that, even though it flows in the Spirit, is a beautiful example of how the apostle Paul said to let everything be done in "decency and order." Pastor Boykin, though a powerful, anointed man of God, doesn't just ask people to come up to the pulpit like that unless God is really speaking to him. Here I was, a twenty-three-year-old young man who now was desperately crying out to God to speak to me and transform my life—and out of nowhere, I heard from the man of God (out of hundreds of people, in a church with an attendance of a couple thousand), "Brother Fred, come up here." As I walked up in a state of shock, Pastor Boykin began to lay hands on me and in lengthy detail prophesied to me of the outstanding and expansive ministry God had prepared for me. From that moment, I preached and operated in an anointing that was very similar to my pastor's. Actually, the way that I teach today in revelation and sound doctrine is all a result of Pastor Boykin. I inherited his character as a family man, a minister of amazing integrity, and a leader of fiery proportions. For eight years I observed every facet of his life, and I can confidently declare to you that I have never seen Pastor Mark David Boykin involved in even one scandal or controversy. These experiences had a profound effect on me and allowed me to know the God of Pastor Boykin.

Then there was Prophet Frank Nattiel. This is the man who taught me how to walk in my office as a prophet, with authority. In a time when I knew I had the calling, but was hesitant to walk in the office fully, he imparted into me confidence in who God anointed me to be.

This was the secret behind Joshua's military victories: the hand of the Lord that was on Moses was also upon him. John the Baptist was the greatest prophet, according to Jesus, but he operated in the mantle of Elijah. You have a destined spiritual DNA. You can receive a mantle in two ways that I see in Scripture. Some receive a mantle by years of service and honor, directly, like Joshua, Elisha, and Timothy did. Others receive a mantle through the sovereignty of God, like John the Baptist, who never met Elijah—but Scripture says he walked in the spirit and power of Elijah. Why go your whole life fighting for elevation to no avail, when you can cross the Jordan River and destroy thirty-one kings and their kingdoms easily, and possess your elevation because of a mantle you've inherited? This is my burden for you, beloved. My burden is that my generation, and the generations after I'm with the Lord, would walk in their elevation worldwide by receiving these prophetic instructions in this book.

I discovered that the hand of the Lord had ten very specific ways it operated in warfare throughout Scripture.

The hand of the Lord released pestilence upon Egypt's livestock

This was the fifth plague of God through Moses, as seen in Exodus 9:2-3 (NKJV). "For if you refuse to let them go, and still hold them, behold, the hand of the Lord will be on your cattle in the field, on the horses, on the donkeys, on the camels, on the oxen, and on the sheep—a very severe pestilence." This is significant because livestock represents the possessions of someone that allow them to both live and survive. For Egypt, it was animals; in today's economy, it's money. When God's hand is upon your life, and you have enemies—whether in the natural or the supernatural—that come against you, God will release this kind of judgment. When a nation is completely away from God, you will see that it affects their economy.

The hand of the Lord releases death

In Exodus 16:3 (NKJV), "And the children of Israel said to them, 'Oh, that we had died by the hand of the Lord in the land of Egypt, when we sat by the pots of meat and when we ate bread to the full! For you have brought us out into this wilderness to kill this whole assembly with hunger.'" The children of Israel acknowledged that the hand of the Lord can take away life. Now, this is not a license to start praying for this to happen to anyone—but biblically, this is what it says. We see in the book of Acts two times that God released this type of judgment in the life of Ananias and Sapphira, and King Herod.

The hand of the Lord destroys all opposition

When the hand of the Lord is on your life, you don't have to lose sleep over your opposition. There will be people who are jealous of you, who want to see you fail, who make things up about you—and believe it or not, even pray against you. Don't be naïve; not everyone wants to see you succeed. Yet you don't have to be afraid, because the hand of the Lord will protect you from all opposition.

The hand of the Lord releases judgment upon witches in churches

I know this may sound strange to you, but read Joshua 22:31 (NKJV): "Then Phinehas the son of Eleazar the priest said to the children of Reuben, the children of Gad, and the children of Manasseh, 'This day we perceive that the LORD is among us, because you have not committed this treachery against the LORD. Now you have delivered the children of Israel out of the hand of the LORD.'" The context of this verse shows that the hand of the Lord would have been against people who were a part of the camp who operated in another spirit or intention. I said "witches in the churches" because witchcraft can be rebellion, control, and manipulation. This is going on in churches all over the world, and you don't have to be afraid of it when the hand of the Lord is on your life.

The calamity of the hand of the Lord can be confused as demonic

In Judges 2:15 (NKJV), "Wherever they went out, the hand of the LORD was against them for calamity, as the LORD had said, and as the LORD had sworn to them. And they were greatly distressed." It speaks of calamity as a result of the hand of the Lord being upon you. Remember, in Amos 3:6 (NKJV) it reads, "If there is calamity in a city, will not the LORD have done it?" The Lord is not limited to what humanity thinks is God. I truly believe that the rulers of nations worldwide would have more respect for men and women of God and the church if they knew this side of the Lord. Not all storms, hurricanes, and tornados are from who you think. We picture God as though He is Mr. Rogers. God's hand is a fearful thing.

The hand of the Lord can close doors that are not part of God's plan

We see this in Ruth 1:13 (NKJV): "Would you wait for them till they were grown? Would you restrain yourselves from having husbands? No, my daughters; for it grieves me very much for your sakes that the hand of Lord has gone out against me." When the hand of the Lord is upon you, He will not allow you to take opportunities that are not His will. He will close doors that you may want opened, and that you even prayed for, but you must trust the hand of the Lord on your life.

The hand of the Lord releases sickness

I know that He is a healer, but 1 Samuel 5:6 (NKJV) shows that God can judge this way as well, and reads as follows: "But the hand of the LORD was heavy on the people of Ashdod, and He ravaged them and struck them with tumors, both Ashdod and its territory." We also know that Paul said that some sleep, or die, by taking communion in an unworthy manner. God controls everything by His divine hand.

When God elevates you, the hand of the Lord is against your enemies your whole life

This is powerful because if you are living, you will have enemies, and many times you don't even know that you have them or who they are. As long as you're living, you are on an assignment. There is no such thing as retiring from your assignment. We see this in 1 Samuel 7:13 (NKJV): "So the Philistines were subdued, and they did not come anymore into the territory of Israel. And the hand of the LORD was against the Philistines all the days of Samuel." You will have victory your entire life when the hand of the Lord is upon you.

The hand of the Lord is not only judgment,
but generational judgment

We see this in 1 Samuel 12:15. There are consequences for coming against God's people and the true leader of the Lord. Many times, we say it's a generational curse, but the Lord releases judgment generationally.

The hand of the Lord upon you will not allow your
enemies to shame you

Finally, in 1 Kings 18:46 (NKJV), "Then the hand of the LORD came upon Elijah; and he girded up his loins and ran ahead of Ahab to the entrance of Jezreel." Elijah ran ahead of Ahab. When God's hand is upon you, not only will you have advantage over your enemies, you will outrun them with exceedingly great speed! God must accelerate you in order to be a testimony against those whom the devil has raised up against you, and by the hand of the Lord you will not be put to shame.

My prayer for you is that, as you ask God to divinely connect you with a true mantle, you would receive a fresh impartation and defeat all the demonic opposition that you will face on your way to your elevation. Let your prayer in this season of your life be that the hand of the Lord would come upon you, that you would operate in supernatural might. No matter where you are right now, get on your knees and open your heart to God with faith and pray this prayer, and receive the hand of the Lord mightily upon your life.

Father God, in the name of Jesus,

May the hand of God come upon me in might, strength, and spiritual violence, that I may destroy every demonic opposition against me on my way to my elevation.

In the name of Jesus,

Amen.

Chapter 4

ENCOUNTERING SUPERNATURAL MIRACLES

Why does it seem that certain individuals experience the miraculous hand of God in their ministries, and others don't? Is it a lack of faith, or is it just that God chooses some to see His miracles, and doesn't choose others? We know for certain that God is no respecter of persons, so what is the missing factor? To adequately answer this question, we must tackle the source of miracles.

First and foremost, miracles are not orchestrated by men; they are done only by God. Though it may seem that a person is performing them, such as Moses lifting up his rod over the Red Sea, it should never be mistaken that his rod or arm was what actually performed the miracle. One of my favorite scriptures is found in Acts 19:11 (NKJV): "Now God worked unusual miracles by the hands of Paul, so that even handkerchiefs or aprons were brought from his body to the sick, and the diseases left them and the evil spirits went out of them." Nowhere does it say that an angel, apostle, or prophet did unusual miracles, but it was God who solely did unusual miracles through the hands of Paul. As great as Paul was, he never did one miracle. So, miracles are contingent upon the decision of God.

There are all kinds of miracles, in many different contexts. Context is more important than the text. The miracles done in the book of Joshua were not random, insignificant miracles. They were supernatural encounters for the elevation of the children of Israel. Here is a principle: the greatest miracles are birthed out of divine purpose. God doesn't just turn water into wine because He's bored! There was a purpose for Christ doing what He did, and it was to confirm His messianic office. Joshua couldn't just wake up and say, "O God, could you just part the Jordan River so I could show Caleb I'm anointed?" There was a purpose for this miracle to be done, and it was done in order for Israel to cross over and possess the Promised Land.

When you position yourself under the mantle of another, and you have not allowed yourself to skip the process due to self-proclaimed exaltation, it now gives the Holy Spirit room to perform the greatest miracles that you will ever see. God will not reward the ambition of self-willed men, as seen in the case of Joshua and Elisha, who trusted the process. Can you name any individuals in Scripture who saw more major miracles than Joshua and Elisha? Think about the enormity of the parting of the Jordan River. First, the Jordan River is the lowest river in the world at 686 feet below sea level, and it is 223 miles long, which would take approximately 72 hours to walk. God used both Joshua and Elisha to part this river. It is not a coincidence that both men were sons of two great fathers in Israel: Moses and Elijah. Though not in name, both surpassed their fathers in works.

This is so important, because many of you reading this book are frustrated by the process of sonship. You look at other peers of yours and wonder why are they making things happen so quickly, while you're here washing Elijah's hands and fighting Moses' battles; while your peers are preaching from place to place, you're over here being an armorbearer to your spiritual father. If this is you, then this chapter is just for you! The hand of the Lord will come upon you to move in the miraculous in your life for one reason amongst many others, which is this: the heaviest anointing for miracles is only reserved for the true sons and daughters of the kingdom. Don't ever equate busyness with a mantle. Don't confuse independence with authority. There are men and women of God who seem like they are doing great moves in the kingdom, because they are busy and are independent of any authority or mantle over their lives from another individual. Consequently, these types of ministries don't experience longevity. This is what's wrong with our present-day prophetic movement. We don't have true major prophets (a Moses or Elijah type of anointing) that have raised up Joshuas and Elishas to walk in longevity. Usually, the ministry lifespan of an influential prophet's ministry in the modern era is not very long. There is a need for proper impartation.

Miracles are effortless for sons and daughters

You will see that Joshua and Moses did not struggle to operate in miracles; it looked almost effortless. The reason is because they saw how God used their spiritual fathers and knew they had that mantle, and thus they operated in confidence. Where God is taking you, it won't be a struggle. However, it will not be easy. You don't have to kill yourself worrying about how you're going to accomplish all of your dreams. Your mantle is your unlimited black card from heaven and the greatest marketer for the projects and assignments you have. Understand that all of Joshua's miracles were effortless. Crossing the Jordan River and the destruction of the walls of Jericho were without human assistance physically.

Certain anointings can only be inherited as a son or daughter

You can't fast and pray that you will receive the spirit of Elijah. It comes in time, and through sonship. There are certain miracles and testimonies that will not be heard by many because they reject authority. There are many who feel that it's a step down to be under a great man of God and to let that mantle or distinct anointing fall upon them. One of the hidden mysteries of receiving a mantle is that it brings you from a place of private insignificance to public prominence. Let me explain. It is vital for you to receive a mantle in order to reach the masses and make an impact in your generation. Pastor Benny Hinn's crowds are too massive to focus on one person getting healed.

Yet, due to his mantle he can set the atmosphere through worship, and see the masses receive their miracles by waving that mantle of Kathryn Kuhlman upon the Jordan River. If you want to encounter supernatural miracles, then wait for your time. I know that it may not be attractive or popular to say in a book like this, or in a conference, but it's biblical. Ask God to lead you to a true apostle's or prophet's ministry, so that you may serve to receive a heavy anointing on your life. This heavy anointing does not come in conferences, but in time.

Miracles depend on your perspective of God

This is such an important section in this book. There are many of you who are walking in someone else's mantle. You have received it either by serving or by the sovereignty of God, and you may not know how to supernaturally operate in that mantle. You may be under a ministry or specific minister, and though you are not walking in the fullness of that anointing, you have that leader's spirit on you—and you want to start seeing some supernatural results. This is a revelation that I have received for you.

Every man or woman of God who has operated in the realm of the supernatural has a specific revelation of who God is to them, and how God wants them to view Him. Though we are to discover who God is as much as possible, when it comes to the supernatural there are certain revelations of God that unleash God's power in a fresh, new way. You will find that God will reveal Himself in very specific ways for specific purposes.

Though I can point out many examples, I would like to focus on Elijah and Elisha. Elijah was as supernatural a prophet as it gets. As a matter of fact, I have titled Elijah, in many of my teachings about him, "a demonstrative prophet." I believe that Moses and Elijah are demonstrative prophets, meaning that they did not only prophesy, but they performed miracles and many signs and wonders by the Spirit of God. Elijah had a mantle that was unique, powerful, and supernatural. He was a mysterious, strange man. It's possible that Elijah lived in the wilderness for most of his life very much like John the Baptist, since John came in the spirit and power of Elijah. Elijah was not recorded as having any friends, so he was a lonely man. All his miracles operated through the spoken word. I believe that he had the New Testament equivalent of the gift of faith. The intensity and violence of his faith led him to confront Ahab the wicked king, and to declare to him, after a deep time of fervent prayer, that there would be a drought for three years. What's interesting is how he addressed God. In 1 Kings 17:1 (NKJV) it says, as Elijah confronts Ahab, "As the LORD God of Israel lives, before whom I stand, there shall be no dew or rain these years, except at my word." Why is it, out of all descriptions, that Elijah called Him Lord before He called Him God? It's because "Lord" in Hebrew means "the self-existent one." That means as Lord, He doesn't have to ask anyone's permission or factor in the impossibilities before He decides supernaturally; He can just do it. It causes you to have faith on a whole other level when you know that you serve a God who can literally do anything on His own, when and how He wants, without any human participation. Do you see God in this way? Have you decided that no matter what the circumstances are, you will only focus on this Lord God?

In all the supernatural works that Elijah did, you will see that he always addressed God as Lord first. When he prophesied to the widow in 1 Kings 17, he addressed God as Lord. When he raised the young boy from the dead in the same chapter, he said in 1 Kings 17:20, "O Lord my God" before he prayed, and the young boy rose from the dead. When Prophet Elijah confronted the 850 false prophets, he said in 1 Kings 18:21 (NKJV), "And Elijah came to all the people, and said, 'How long will you falter between two opinions? If the LORD is God, follow

Him; but if Baal, follow him.' But the people answered him not a word." Immediately thereafter, as you already know, one of the most unusual signs and wonders took place. Fire came down from heaven to consume the sacrifices. Elijah focused on God as Lord. The One who controlled everything—including the climate, supernatural elements in heaven, multiplication of resources, and even life in a dead boy. Do you see God like that today? This must be the focus of your prayer life, studies, and ministry, if you want to see these kinds of miracles.

As soon as Elisha received the mantle from Elijah, the first thing he did was to go to the Jordan River and strike the river, declaring in 2 Kings 2:14 (NKJV), "Where is the LORD God of Elijah?" This was not by mistake; this was Elisha learning the prophetic secret of knowing and believing God as Lord.

This principle is not only limited to knowing God as Lord. No matter the calling you have upon your life, you must pray and ask God how He wants you to perceive Him in your ministry assignment. If you do a study of great men of God, you will see that they discovered that God was either a Healer, a Deliverer, a good God, or not an angry God all the time. Their revelation of God was the driving force of their ministry. The question I would ask any general in the kingdom of God who has a powerful mantle on their life is, "Who is God to you, predominantly?" As you pray intensely to God, seek Him for fresh new revelation of who He is; let that be the theme of your ministry, and watch how God uses you.

The level of your encounter with God privately is the level of your miracles publicly

You will see that before God started to use certain men in the Bible, God would visit them one on one, in a very real way. I remember the way I received the baptism of the Holy Spirit. God visited me, and I had a beautiful vision of the throne of

God, and the altar of God was so white that I cannot even explain it; and the next thing I knew was that I started to release my heavenly language. Another time I was praying at midnight, and I was seeking God with all that was in me, and all of a sudden I felt someone gently make me get on my face, prostrate before God, to worship Him. There have been times in prayer at night when I have been caught in realms of the Holy Spirit, when all I could do was weep like a baby because of the very sweetness of the encounter with His Spirit—there's just too many to name. Many times, I would feel tangible fire on my body, and it would just bring me to tears and brokenness. Many times, I would find myself during deep intercessory prayer, and the Spirit of God would come upon me and I would be praying, but almost fighting as I'm praying. I believe this is due to the wrestling with principalities and powers and rulers of the darkness of this age and spiritual hosts of wickedness in heavenly places.

Therefore, pray! You spend alone time with God so that you can have experiences and encounters with God that produce real miracles and supernatural acts of the power of God. It's not enough to read this book; you must use this book as fuel for you to seek God. I challenge you to obey God by going on a fast when the Holy Spirit leads you; spend deep and long times of prayer with God to have your personal encounter with His Spirit. Do not let the ministry hijack your personal time with God. Before you minister, shut down all activities and seek the Lord uninterruptedly until you meet Him. This will cause you to operate in the supernatural at greater levels. If you don't have many opportunities to minister, don't complain; take this time to have alone time and experiences with Him that will enlarge the capacity of the supernatural in your ministry. In communicating this to you, I feel the fire of the Spirit. I prophesy over your life that this is a season of you encountering His precious Spirit. There is an anointing on this book, and the rea-

ou have this book in your hands is because God is longing
isit you. The Spirit of the Lord doesn't want us to com-
nicate with a God in public that we have not encountered
in private. The gifts inside of you can only awaken and not
remain dormant if you are in the presence of the same Spirit
that raised Jesus from the dead. This is why your ministry has
not produced the supernatural results that you desire. It's not
in the style of preaching or the sound of your voice, but in the
encounter you have privately. What you experience privately
will determine what you see supernaturally occur in public.

It's in private that you learn to be sensitive to the Holy Spirit.
In these alone times you learn His voice; you learn how He
uses you and deals with you. God doesn't deal with any two
people the same. You learn how He speaks to you in these precious moments. What a wonderful Lord we serve! To allow us
to know Him this way is worth more than money. Your public
ministry is just an overflow of your private ministry. As you
keep this principle, you will last in ministry and go from glory
to glory.

My prayer for you is that this book pushes you into private
times of encounters and experiences with God—your God.
Follow the kingdom principles of this book, and you will see
your life transform to another level. Senior pastors, teach this
book to your members and leaders. May this book be taught
in conferences all over the world, that God's order would be
back in the body of Christ. There have been many of you who
have been hurt by spiritual fathers in the past, and the devil
has attacked you this way so the revelation of this book cannot
be followed in your life. Don't minister from a hurt and bitter
place. Forgive that leader, and anyone who has ever hurt you,
and get in your proper alignment and position yourself as a son
or daughter. There are mantles that are hanging in the Spirit,
ready to fall on you, all over the world. You cannot reach the
level you desire without a mantle, or heavy distinct anointing,

and the principles of this book will bring you from a Mantle to Manifestation, Might, and finally to Miracles. It's yours, and from this day I declare over your life that as you receive the revelation from this book, your life will never be the same, in Jesus' name.

About the Author

From Prophet Fred Louis's conception in his mother's womb, the enemy sought to hijack and abort his destiny before he came to full term. However, in God's sovereignty He overruled, overturned, and dismissed every demonic assignment—because before He formed him, He knew him; before he was born, He sanctified him; and ordained him as a prophet to the nations. Therefore, let me introduce to you this first-generation preacher and well sought-after speaker, who ministers the rightly divided Word of God with dynamic authority and like a mighty rushing wind. His powerful presentation of the gospel has enabled Prophet Fred Louis to minister to many multitudes across the globe. He has traveled extensively throughout the United States and abroad in such countries as Haiti, where he preached to over 16,000 people—not including the hundreds and thousands of listeners on the radio. Also, he's preached in the Bahamas and the Dominican Republic.

Answering the call and surrendering his life to Jesus Christ as his Lord and Savior in July, 2005, at Church of All Nations under the leadership of Pastor Mark D. Boykin, immediately after his conversion he entered Bible school at the International School of Ministry due to his unyielding passion for spreading the liberating Word of God. As a result, he has left an immeasurable impact by his thought-provoking, revelatory, and prophetic teaching of the gospel of Jesus Christ. His uniqueness and anointing have become a signature trademark of his intelligent and articulate delivery of the Word. As a man of profound faith, Prophet Fred Louis walks in truth and integrity, and operates in a combined prophetic and teaching mantle. Due to his exuberant love for the Word of God, after he finished Bible school he became a licensed pastor under

Christian Ministries International in 2007, and was ordained in 2009. Subsequently, being diligent in serving other departments with a proven track record of being successful in various leadership roles, Prophet Fred was appointed as co-associate director of the Bible school which he attended, later renamed The Fire Institute.

Prophet Fred Louis has become a recognized prophetic voice and a Pentecostal charismatic preacher/leader, releasing the unrelenting rhema word. His radical, bold approach and ability to break down complex revelation into simplistic terms has spread like wildfire among the masses!

Prophet Fred Louis has the instrumental capability, being equipped by the Holy Spirit in demonstration and power, to demoralize and demolish the strongman and strongholds operating behind the scenes through his prophetic insight into the Spirit realm. There has been a demonstration of working of miracles and gifts of healing of cancer and paralysis under the unction of the Holy Spirit while he's ministered. Through the empowerment of the Holy Spirit, he has been able to release divine impartation of the manifestations of the Holy Spirit. Meanwhile, during his altar calls, there has been an unveiling of the supernatural being released in the atmosphere where waves of glory have shifted churches and cities.

He's been married to his beautiful queen and right-hand woman, Prophetess Naomi Louis, since 2012. Together they are joyful parents of a beautiful boy named Joel Louis. Though committed to the vision God has given him to lead the ministry, his greatest burden is the legacy of his family. His biggest dream was to be married not only to a godly woman, but to his ministry teammate; as a result, this gave birth to Team Louis Ministries. As said many times by Prophet Fred Louis, "The vision of Team Louis Ministries began in my heart when I was single and crying to God for the kind of ministry, wife, and family I desired. Team Louis is a prophetic word that the wife and seed of the Louis's will walk in the greatness of Christ, and together reach the world by the power of the Holy Ghost."

CPSIA information can be obtained
at www.ICGtesting.com
Printed in the USA
LVHW080230160520
655580LV00005B/1043